Music From Words

MUSIC FROM WORDS

Marc Jampole

Bellday Books, Inc.
Durham, North Carolina

© 2007 by Marc Jampole
First Printing

Published by Bellday Books, Inc., P.O. Box 37, Durham, NO, 27702;
www.belldaybooks.com

"Music from Words,"
Cover and interior design by Cassandra Patten.

Library of Congress Cataloguing-in-Publication Data

Jampole, Marc, 1950-
   Music from words: poems / Marc Jampole.
     p. cm.

   ISBN 978-0-9793376-0-4

1. Americans-Poetry. I. Title.
Library of Congress Control Number 2007922168

For Leslie

ACKNOWLEDGEMENTS

Grateful acknowledgement goes to the following journals in which these poems initially appeared, sometimes in earlier drafts:

Oxford Review: "July Fourth"; Oxford Review nominated "July Fourth" for The Pushcart Prize.

Mississippi Review: "Dot and Sylvia"

Pittsburgh Quarterly: "The Death Song of Lenny Ross"

Janus Head: "These are a Few"

Paper Street: "Showing off the Roses"

Negative Capability: "Moses in the Suburbs"

Ellipsis: "Liana to Rafflesia"

MUSIC FROM WORDS
Table of Contents

I. Operas and Arias

3   July 4th
4   Dot and Sylvia
6   The Death Song of Lenny Ross
10   These are a Few
12   Showing off the Roses
15   Thomas Alfred Thinks About His Princesses
19   Moses in the Suburbs
21   Hugo Speaks to Himself and Emmy Speaks to Hugo
24   Remember the Fool in the Rain

II. Love Songs

29   Afternoon on the Island (After Seurat)
30   Liana to Rafflesia
31   Maya
32   A Brief Thought to its Mistress
33   I Want to Know You Five Ways
34   Yes and Know

III. Abstract Music

39   Source Of All
43   Squaw Valley Lodgepole Pine
44   Imaginary Landscape with 29 Birds
49   Outside a Snowscape
51   Weather is the Only Proof
53   Pascal's Triangle

IV. Protest Rock

57   Staff Meeting Minutes
58   What about the Losers?
60   Dreams of Old Men
62   Ghost
64   Gilgamesh in a Traffic Jam
66   A Dream of Post-Historic Times
67   Faith is a Fine Invention
69   Variations on a Ballad

V. Songs of Self

77   Again in L. A.
78   Apollo
80   The Sixth Dream of Gilgamesh
81   Ravings of an Atheistic Stylite
83   Schoenberg's Second Conversion
84   One of Repin's Volga Boatmen

87   Notes

Operas and Arias

July 4th

And the three-year-old at the picnic
said she wanted to play the violin
and I said, just like Joe Venuti
and she said, you're a Joe Venuti
and I said, you're a Joe Venuti
and she pulled a tuft of grass and said,
here's some Joe Venuti
and she pointed to a sparrow scratching in the dust
and said, there's a Joe Venuti
and from a plastic bag she dumped
a bunch of Joe Venutis
and barbecue flames caressed the grilling Joe Venutis
and men threw the Joe Venuti, popping their gloves,
while women slurped the Joe Venuti and spit the seeds
and the sun played hide and seek in dissipating Joe Venutis
and through poplar branches Joe Venuti shadows danced
across the baby's sleeping smile.

Later, like Marcus Aurelius
observing models of human behavior,
we watched the ducks glide away
after the bread was gone.

Dot and Sylvia

Both plunged beads of boiling fudge through frigid water
at the perfect point, without thermometer,
beat egg and air with effortless wrist spins,
created endless games with plastic dinosaurs
and pieces of paper on rainy afternoons,
peeled fruit for all children and adults she loved,
fell to knees in mock anger and pointed index finger
to emphasize a discrepancy in height,
played Stravinsky and Carmen with Leontyne Price,
taught children funny words to the Toreador Song,
listened tenderly as others told their lives,
loved to talk about books she read,
to feel big wet drops fall on her hair and face in an open field,
to close eyes and imagine making love
to the warm flat stone on which she was sunning,
wanted a strong and brilliant male to obliterate her
then hated him for doing so,
spoke often of what others thought of her
of what they thought she thought they thought,
stewed about public snubs that no one else could see,
said nasty things when she couldn't hold her liquor,
would suddenly turn on others, then seek forgiveness,
requested permission to loathe her mother,
mouthed troubling phrases:
stasis in darkness
the brown arc
the dew that flies
she never loved me
he touched me in that spot,

4

fluctuated between loving every stranger
and abhorring her own flesh,
savored jolt after jolt of current
piercing her body like a lover gone wild,
stayed in bed by day, paced halls by night,
found it easier to remember
moments of gloom than moments of radiance,
examined several forms of suicide
until selecting one, and here they differed:
Sylvia stuck her head in an oven.
Dot swallowed pills.

The Death Song of Lenny Ross

*Lenny Ross was a Whiz Kid quiz show contestant as a child in the 50's who
later became an advisor to Jerry Brown and held several academic positions.*

Dow's theory analyzes market action.
Fundamentals deal in corporate prospects.
When stocks are good, T-bills suffer,
and when the market shakes its head and shoulders,
it's time to sell, or buy.

What a boy you are, Lenny Ross, Lenny Ross!
What a genius boy you are!
And why not you, Lenny?
Why not you to win the hundred thousand
answering quiz-show questions
on stocks and bonds and whatever?
Why not you the youngest?
At five you talked like Walter Lippmann.
At six you built a TV by yourself!
What a boy you are, Lenny!
What a genius boy you are!

Our tort system, from English common law,
changes many features of that older land's.
The principle's the same,
that assets yield to no man save one who has them.
Eschewing class, we're guided by associations,
men maintaining liberty by joining others openly,
as Tocqueville described, recalling Edmund Burke.

He grasped all aspects of the reading,
wrestling levels none of us had thought about,
as we sat silent, listening to his playfulness
with concepts none of us had heard before.
And yet so kind he was to all of us, his elders,
so patient telling us his thoughts.
What a mind he had, Lenny Ross,
and what a knowledge of the law.

A head that talks, an academic side man,
I know that's what they think of me.
Great idea, Lenny! What a brain!
I want to be a man of action, commanding heads of state
I want to run for President one day.
I have a master plan.
It's all up here!

Slow down, Lenny Ross, finish one thing!
I told him that a thousand times, at least,
then watched him stagger back and forth
among his shriveled plants and dusty chairs,
popping frozen peas at open mouth
and throwing out ideas like cannon shot.
And it was up to me to understand
that he had skipped ahead to chapter five.
Slow down, Lenny! I can't keep up.
But he persisted with a logic of his own.

Here's the plan:
We'll write a treatise on the rights of students
and with the money earned, we'll buy these artists:

Fieldes, Moore and Greaves;
minor works by minor painters.
By lending them to small museums,
their values will inflate,
and then we sell and start a franchise.

I knew his reputation: Fired from Harvard,
bewildered students, uncompleted books.
But those first flowing days in Sacramento,
those synergistic days!
We watched him use a roll of tape and scissors
to cut and splice my program.
The spaceship earth, the new age economics,
the art of Zen applied to government....
It was all there.
If things had turned out different, Lenny Ross,
you would have been my Commerce Secretary.

A six-month freeze on wages
without a freeze on prices,
followed by a year of frozen subsidies,
after which we send a thousand troops to Spain
as warning to the Sheiks to drop the price of oil.
I'll send the President a memorandum
when I've wrapped my piece on Masons.
It's full of great ideas.

Don't call me anymore, Lenny Ross,
I've had about enough of you
and your constant chatter leading nowhere.
You can't keep quiet long enough to love me.
You touch my thigh, then start to babble economics,
then write a sentence down, then phone a friend,
remember I'm in bed and ask me
what I think of Bergman's latest flick.

8

I can't take it anymore, Lenny Ross!
Genius, shit! Just get it up and keep it up for once!

A thermo coupler made of fiberglass
Kabuki language representing social graces
Venture funds investing in technology
In five years' time, the baby boomers will
Stendhal's real name was
Juan Gris merely described what he
Sawmills replacing windmills along the Flemish...

You're back home, Lenny,
and we'll take care of you.
No more taking jobs and quitting three months later.
No more lying under cars reciting lectures.
You'll rest awhile, Lenny, and then you'll see.
You'll land a cushy job.

...theory of addled value William Cullen
Randolph the red-nosed option underlying
Tinto Ramm Dass vodanya Montana the Puritan
migraine persecution of the Cotton Mather
tell Jerry my name is Gemini
Carter Wilson Picket the symbol of an angry
zero coupon to beat the plowshares into Isaiah Berlin...

My voice now, Lenny,
my voice calm, first time in years,
looking through the waters of the Capri Motel pool,
hearing waves applaud with plastic hands,
smelling chlorine smoke, tasting acrid starlight fruit.
Jump, Lenny Ross.
Remove this yoke of expectation.
Jump, Lenny,
jump to freedom...

These are a Few

Last night in sheets of sound I sweated junky harmony:
slick streets, lights moving darkness, silence like clamor,
void where needle pierces into skin, into nerve, into mind,
rain drops on roses, stillness with whiskers, droplets are snare drums
throbbing sweet wonders, copper kettles, mittens, ecstatic seeking,
brown paper packages tied up in veins, door bells and sleigh bells
in trees, cicadas are legato mallets that understand the universe

as jagged metal tone, a loss of binding chordal sense, witch pitch,
cat walk, wringing sheets dripping sweat and urine,
wringing sound from dripping pages, extracting music,
vomiting green excreta of my favorite things, my favorite notes,
my favorite girls in white dissonance, bitter tastes pour past open lips,
sweet tastes stream past the rush at unexpected withdrawal
when my man came with blue satin sashes, snowflakes that stayed,

the rush at playing the unexpected interval, the completed scale,
every music resonates that bursting spirit of sleep, resonates
restless modality, something I dreamed last night flushes warm
like bright copper kettles melting in needle's first fire inside,
wild geese fly above the Hudson, cream colored ponies, schnitzel
with noodles ripping at liver, diseased flesh my spirit's home,
like the tenor tone that stays inside, silver-white winters

that melt in dry mouth, arms too heavy to lift, brain thrashes
cold goose bumps, restlessness, bone and muscle cramps,
is this how my father died in his stomach? how my aunt and others?
bus rumbling past window, pestilent street lamp through
cracks between blind and sill beaming like deadly heaven,
was it at the Vanguard with those white eyelashes wearing suede?
was it in that room without chairs? was it with cream colored peonies

where I blew long trills through collapsing veins, briskly opened
to journey beyond all of them, beyond all questions,
something that hasn't been played before, the moon my crescent,
its wing my meditation, sings supreme silence, giant steps,
from the first sound all history unfolding as lotus, the central hub
from which voices are spokes in the first vibration, the eyelash,
implacable, unmovable legs, heart slowing to walking bass beat

in a ballad of acknowledgement, resolution, pursuance, psalm,
the speaker obliterated in his own sounds, the left hand rising,
intangible resembling tangible, wandering through sacred grounds
in this city at night, the train's rumble like the horn in my head,
the river within the thing and the thing within itself, the thing waking,
the thing dreaming, the thing in dreamless sleep, forming eternal
mouth moves and makes no sound, then sound of soundlessness,

then remembrance of sound, chant grabbing yellowing skin,
when I'm feeling sad I simply remember the warm woolen
vamp of change, these are a few of my favorite tones,
no such thing as dying young except for those I leave behind
in brown paper packages tied with the chant that's a habit,
the chant that's a dream, the chant that's a meditation of the sound
listening for it all the time in everything, not finding it and still I search.

Showing off the Roses

Move slowly,
    see everything, always saw everything, always saw.
More time now,
    pushing muscles pushing back, more time now.
Show plants and bushes,
    dirt bulge like sponge cake round small ceramic ladies.
Then have lunch,
    search for legs, stopped inside my frozen moment,
embarrassed by this stiff,
    slow sadness. Would show you every flower
but you came
    two weeks early, nothing but tight green buds,
Royal Bonica,
    Boule de Neige, Candelabra, Morden Fireglow,
other names too slow to open,
    all have stories after lunch, after cake,
after drift,
    after pink and red unravel.
In that row
    Gold Medals grow. Later we'll play
Benny Goodman.
    Fifty-three bushes, rose details:
in that row
    Gold Medals grow, First Light, French Lace.
Always saw everything,
    never had to say because I was the good boy,

with the good head,
  the good study, the good reward, the stained *substantia nigra.*
Without twinge,
  without sever it happened, my secret,
Benny Goodman
  always made me sad. Now the slow squeal exhausts
and the sadder not-roses,
  amaryllis and birds of paradise, forget this other.
Can't bend to grab
  that weed, would petrify, sound on plastic.
You need that twisted
  piece of metal tool.
Try it with fingers
  while I move the other foot,
roots and dirt.
  Slide my hip toward the walker,
toward the mulberry.
  About the amaryllis, what do you mean
it wasn't Benny Goodman?
  It was drift, bleak slowness then eruption of tremble,
lava limbs
  blasting from my torso, but you won't see.
Good boys are slow,
  careful, recommend Benny Goodman.

Dug these

    years ago, Boule de Neige, Royal Bonica.

Someone else

    mows and clips, not Benny Goodman.

Lift my right leg

    near the walker. Go to lunch and yellow cake.

Take my pills

    in three hours. Let's stop here.

Soon complete

    the trek across the grass and patio.

Only the good boy

    gets sweets, ravish the cake,

flay it with the spoon,

    carefully balance the sweet yellow quiver,

take it to the lips,

    chew it for days, because I am still the good boy.

Thomas Alfred Thinks About His Princesses

Heading north,
Thomas Alfred starts and stops,
alone like other drivers
and thinks of chops for dinner —
his latest dream — home-fried onions
glazed and gracing sizzling pork,
not the crispy greasy battered rings
his princess said she's bringing home
with fries and chicken nuggets.

Heading north, Thomas Alfred thinks
of evening peace in TV sports,
the soothing click between three games
until he enters snore, and then her shake,
If you're sleepy, go to bed,
which makes him think, the creaky cot,
their starter house some years ago,
when she would purr, Tom, be a tom,
and let him have her anytime he liked.
Did she fake it then like she fakes it now?
every other week before her latest fusillade,
Tom, be a dear, let's do the kitchen,
this year, not next. Rates are low
so now's the time, brand-new floor,
let's make the counter lime.

Heading north, Thomas Alfred recollects
that he has children somewhere
in the township, kicking soccer balls,
hanging out in malls, or maybe home
chatting electronically, as he at work
with princess EVP of sales, *Tom be a saint,*
take my morning meeting, show restraint
when they ask us for concessions.
Negotiate, stone the wall, report:
there's a dream he had one night
and realizes every day.

Heading north, Thomas Alfred craves
the scooped-neck blouse she wears
from time to time revealing sixteen freckles
on one side of the great divide,
her lean across the conference table
showing more. Is it inadvertent
when she crosses legs too slowly?
He knows he's not supposed to look,
but puffy white is there to see
at her vertex for the fraction of an instant:
subtle gesture of availability
or flaunt of various powers?
He knows he'll never know
because he'll never try to know.

Heading north, Thomas Alfred writes
in mind a letter he will send
as *tomtomtom-at-a-o-l*
by email to eight names
he hopes are lovely princesses.
He never asks for photographs
which might destroy his fantasy
when posts allude to certain practices
best performed when nude,
and he'll refrain from asking for a lunch,
afraid the name might know his princess wife
or be a man or princess daughter's friend,
or have a scar that makes it hard to conjure lust.

Heading north, Thomas Alfred hears
the hourly news on radio invade
his private brood of closer troubling matters,
the guillotine of bills, deadlines that intrude
on email love affairs, that swill
he has to drink before his colonoscopy,
the latest row between his princess wife
and princess daughter, hiss and spit
back and forth all night about her clothes
from golden pedestals erected
each in separate corners of the living room,
or was that fix-it feat another dream?

Driving north, Thomas Alfred contemplates
his current state, how he has landed
at that instant on that more traveled road.
He never thought to take another way,
rung by rung a careful climb,
each step the one his father took
and princess mother said was best,
and yes, it's good, career and home and kids
and countless princesses for mall-walk stares
or brief communiqués of cloudy promise,
yet at times he wants to fall asleep
in traffic, let his forehead plummet
onto leather steering wheel
or into pile of whipped potatoes
in a Dalton serving bowl on Saturdays
when in-laws come for princess roast beef,
wake up years from now, see the indentation
in the creamy mash of white
hardened to a mask of expectation.

Moses in the Suburbs

And he looked across the wilderness and saw
cars grazing in rows on asphalt patches
and others lulling in carports, Volvos and SUVs
and he felt himself a stranger.
And along his own swatch of grass
children shot imaginary rays at giggling robots.
And inside, his wife was using
the sushi maker or the trash compactor,
he wasn't sure which, but he heard the whir
and it smote him like a slave master's club against a stranger.
And the boy was in the carport waxing his surfboard
and the girl was running water
and curling her hair with an electric comb
and he smirked: he owned two
because his children wanted newer ones with super watts
and granted older ones to strangers.
And on his desk piled contracts for other ranch oases.
He bought and sold them like flocks of sheep.
And in this wilderness he saw a burning bush
and he cried out, Here I am.
And he took off his Nikes,
walked past ray-shooting children,
Dad, Dad, duck the evil Empire!
and he cried again, Here I am,
and floated toward the burning bush.
And his wife was at the door, cell phone in hand,
calling them for lunch, microwave-heated canned soup.
And she saw him walk barefoot through desert's burning coals
and she asked him when he was buying a new printer.
And he said, Here I am,

and stopped at the burning bush
and bowed his head.
Dear, what are you doing at the fire hydrant?
Come, have some lunch!
Here I am.
And the bush answered,
The people suffer and they don't even know it.
Dear, come have some lunch!
You're giving me a headache standing there
and we're out of Tylenol.
They are happy in their suffering.
You must take away their happiness so they understand.
But they won't listen.
I will make them listen.
Listen to me dear, is something wrong?
And she walked to the fire hydrant, hand-fanning.
Gee, it's hot! I'm glad of central air!
And he slapped her face
in front of the burning bush
and it was the face of a stranger.
And he went to the carport and took the gas can
and scattered gas along the siding.
One match and it was burning more brightly
than even the burning bush.
And he turned to his pyre
and bowed his head and said,
Here I am.

Hugo Speaks to Himself and Emmy Speaks to Hugo

How do you feel gnawing on bread
bought with money earned by pimping
your uncovered wife to soldiers
in a wilted precinct in a war-time city?

> *Our rules:*
> *I never enjoy it.*
> *You never ask me if I did.*

When you make love to her,
do you think of your biscuit
slathered with butter?

> *At least you're not a walking dead,*
> *howling in a military hospital,*
> *or limping on the street*
> *foot crutch foot crutch crumple crutch,*
> *or limpless zombie haunting nighttime showers.*

Is this the reason why in dreams
a faceless man sucks your penis?

> *Everything is good and just to god.*
> *Only for men are some things not.*

A burning for call and response,
lawless simplicity, flight from trepanned time,
the law of chance triumphant.

Let's live beyond this daily world:
an inner emigration, self-imposed.

Electromagnetic spider webs

undercover soothing movement

cable tracks on mustard gas

together hit and run

smoking tank trapped and frying

let us make a meal of it

anima mundi escapes the machine

come bathe in woman's tongue

confiscated gnats and smoking butterflies

a silence breathing you and me

bunker tallow thatch

warmly

furrow hidden

harmonious

flown away

emerging, merging

demented apparatus

together circling

dreamless streets

twine of kindling flesh

owls of peace

touch and break apart.

Remember the Fool in the Rain

Rows and rows of water bullets
wobbling, coiling, looping through
impulsive wind across a field,
every drop a transient soul
in steady flood from sun and cloud.
Madman washes clothes he wears
sockless sneakers, shredded denims,
rainbow tee shirt, busted glasses,
greasy, pockmarked, long-haired point of fragile coil:
blinded seer, clever jester, drunken mentor,
the stutterer with the magic staff,
Amos as he first appeared to Northern tribes,
cranky, sloppy, forecasting impossible doom,
Cassandra, ranting royal beauty crawling
through marl from her own family's ridicule,
buckled, shrunken philosoph in rags,
Epictetus slave, Francois Hobo,
Don Quixote, Long John Silver,
hairless Gandhi marching salt to sea,
the clown who reads my fortune.

The madman bays at clouds,
all his wisdom coalesced
to slithering aphorism:
the source of things is rod in ground
tell earth surrounded river never
stays the same reflections having cave and tiny
matter putrefies through present hidden
has lost his brutish restless yearning speaks
his exit leap the sentimental flops on jack
kick sings an opposite and equal light

refracts to rebirth of spirit marching
through architectonics that stumbling you
over pebbles building fractions burning
defeated angels under concrete paradigm
universals needed black hole seeded
and nickel fickles tickling crime
with stickling ideations, pickled velvet
every act a Satyagraha every word a....

Unwritten genius disappears,
abyss of mounting graveyard
or greasy pockmarked folklore.
We outside his corpse soon follow,
we who chant his words soon follow,
we who clutch his face soon follow,
we who we who we who we,
will soon will soon will soon who we,
will soon who we, will soon who we,
will soon who we will soon who we will soon,

who we will soon.

It's good to know the rain will fall
many times again before I die.

Love Songs

Afternoon on the Island
(After Seurat)

In a distance I see her,
past families with dogs, couples under trees,
beyond a trumpet player, last drops of rain
among shadows with concrete hardness

in an instant of harmonious motion, I see her
and the scene parses into stillness of one part
of one part of one part of a moment when
objects transform to trembling specks of color

as when someone's talking through the night
and through persistent tiredness you hear
hypnotic human drone, your vision fractured
into bits of unrelated matter, I see her
behind the patchwork yellow, patchwork green,
patchwork walkers, idlers, runners, butterfly,

in a hard-bustled dress, fitted bodice,
I see her colors swimming into orange,
pink hydrangea oval brimming hat,
looking at the rowers in the river
then turning towards me, smiling,

a woman I could love, or think of loving,
the thought like swarms of little dots
of color holding phrases holding words
holding phonemes holding elemental sounds,
confused and orderly, soothing, disconcerting,
wholes and parts, ordained and accidental,
as love is always, a new way of seeing,
a new way of not seeing.

Liana to Rafflesia

And still I love you,
rootless, leafless, stemless parasite.

Your filaments entwine inside me, vegetate,
migrate to my woody skin, form a knot.

The knot becomes a bud becomes a globe
becomes a russet cabbage slowly swelling
becomes enormous leathered flower,
vermillion petals stretching a meter.

Stamen and pistil embrace, create
a white corona at your center
seven splendid days until you shrivel,
plummet from my bark to steamy jungle floor.

And still I climb the lower slopes
in love with you as you deplete me,
as I deplete you, be your rafflesia
and you as my liana, letting me
suck life inside your vine,
complete my blooming
in and on your body.

Our parasitic sport
becomes our need becomes our love.

Maya

Afterwards my gloom observes you
gather floor-strewn tumulus of clothes.
The bathroom light reveals a passing wraith,
spectral furnishings and photographs that knit
at once to shaft of light, compress to darkness.
Muffled water arrows pound an unseen slurry.
What lie this time—long lines, wrong turn?
Will he smell me on your body?
Will he lacerate your qualms with blissful chatter
when you push his wheelchair, spoon him soup,
climb inside the chores of cleaning up a war?
I am sieve you comb through sand in search
of tender, vital jinnis. And at that fragile burst,
in that isogloss between conceived and real,
mist of golden pooling in your lap,
swan-dive open wing enflaming overhead,
were you with me or with him
with someone else or by yourself?
The water stops, the door unlocks unsettled light
like a man who's run away from thoughts.

A Brief Thought to Its Mistress

Let's pretend that I exist,
pretend I breathe, pretend I'm here,
pretend I touch exactly where you want me to,
pretend I move to where you want my touch to be
as free will not as paratonic loving,
slower ambling closed encircle,
real as dream, palpable as smoke.

Let's pretend that you exist,
pretend you breathe, pretend you're here,
pretend you stop exactly where I want you to,
pretend you turn to where I want your gaze to fall
as weighted wanton naiad, not as fantasy,
slower floating open mouth,
real as flame, tangible as song.

Let's pretend that we're pretending
to jump together hand in hand
toward dark abyss pretending it's a lighted way.

If a mistress thought reveals herself in colors,
yours are antique hues unfolding
into glowing beryl foils and velvet veins
pretending to flutter an aging embrace
as cats pretend attack: conceal, reveal,
present, withdraw, remember, smile,
pretend prehensile grace, pretend surprise,
real as smoke, palpable as dream.

I Want to Know You Five Ways

Jains believe that there are five kinds of knowledge: 1) physical; 2) mental;
3) through words; 4) clairvoyant; and 5) omniscient in the present, past and future.

Soft-shell breathing, oboe voice,
emanations pebbly cold,
balmy warm, crimson blush,
fragrant ambit brush of skin

and inward smiling silent
reading, morning meditation,
yen for bread and fish eggs,
worry, sense of well-being

only known as words
river wide mountain high
heart for body, vein of rock
as green of leaf grasps sunlight

not there but still there
your thereness always there
over where your thereness
senses there in thereness

the everything of your everything
omnipresent in all present
future past of passion's
future past and present passion.

Yes and Know

Yes me don't yes me
know me don't know me
know the moving blue
know the scent of flesh.

Play me don't play me,
play with me don't play
play triste but briskly paced
play *allegro vivace*, play *in medias res.*

Touch me don't touch me
touch me in that place
don't place me in that touch
don't punch me with your'hunches
punch me gently with your shadow.

Shadow my ways don't shadow my ways
way-find my yesterdays don't ask
ask me anything ask me why
don't ask me why your shadows glow.

Fabricate my flesh don't
fabricate my mind don't
fabricate today fabricate
the sun moon sway don't sway
don't look away look inside
don't look inside look away don't look.

Don't let me stop you stop me
don't stop me don't stop
don't stop thinking
think about stopping
think about not stopping
you can stop whenever you like
don't stop till I say to, stop.

Abstract Music

Source of All

"...but Thales says it is water."
Aristotle, Metaphysics

I.
Water is as water does
flows falls splashes freezes
blesses drips and droplets
swells sinuous see-through gray

> Water flows blesses swells
> is fallen drips sinuous
> as splashes and see-through
> water freezes droplets gray.

Fog over fields and ponds
but clear on tire warmed
highway red dawn tinges
avens yellow bedstraw agrimony

> Fog but highway avens
> over clear red yellow
> fields on dawning bedstraw
> ponds warm tinges agrimony.

Anemone soldiers tendriled under
water battle caste of pawn
fringes no man's land
deadlocked pallid benthic imprints

Anemone water fringes deadlocked
soldiers battle no pallid
tendriled cast of man's benthic
under pawning landed imprints.

Water is as water does
Water flows blesses swells
Fog over fields and ponds
Fog but highway avens
Anemone soldiers tendriled under
Anemone water border deadlocked.

II.
Once believed water
became earth became fire
became air became water
tried to mutate gold from lead
thought life sprang from dung on impulse
watched the sun and stars revolve around the earth.

Where do we go from here?
Under water under welkin under tendriled tent
of falling blossoms wearing fog at once believed
a sign a sign of something
transcendence or the law of condensation
connections to connections to connections
another form of water
sometimes river sometimes puddle
sometimes crystal cleaving to a golden shard of leaf

sometimes sadness weeding healthy plants
sadness falling blossoms sadness melting snow field
sadness arms around the dead in photos
sadness wears their songs and movies
        sadness all was and will be.

III.
Water is as water does.

Porous sheen of light in amber
raveled contrail tinting sky
tendriled bedstraw yellow
lifting fog blue water
border clear red highway.

        In the beginning is the beginning
        of the beginning of the beginning.
        At the end of the end is the end of the end.

Sadness fogging stand in water
confuses faith in is and is
discolored blurring disembodied as
was or will be water does.

        Sad confused discolor was
        fogging faith blurring will
        standing is in disembodied being
        water is as water does.

IV.

Another form of water
sharing clear field vision
downpour sweeping towards us
marching pallid water soldiers
skimming over crumbled stumps
towards us flowing falling
splashes porous sheen
towards us earth sink ponding
and beating avens yellow bedstraw
above us tendriled contrail welkin
descending blossoms mutate impulse
together seeing it together
at the beginning and at the end
for once the same sinuous something
another form of water was and will be
another form of water is and is.

Squaw Valley Lodgepole Pine

Above a pluckline blue
     I am pine am male am female

          dangle brown-nub male-waft pollen
              female open gnome-cone cluster

          lodgepole-blown upward dust thermal roam
      lodgepole to nowness pine conespread seek

captured isness under edgepoint
     slicehome branchroot indwell

          safe from squirrel gnaw through
              pinelove frenzy nowness.

          Shelter union lodgepole
     dropping dirtward open

subsisting dome in slot-spike swarm
     mold-nameless veil now-fungus barb.

          Needle-couple lichen harbor.
              Pine thirst after loam terrain

          water measure titrate
     nowness union isness

pinehome living male and female I am.

Imaginary Landscape with 29 Birds
(After Audubon)

Reptile stalking snake legs balance
whiter feather arching cruelty ending eyes
black-brown scissors poking after lizard slither.

Hooping Crane

Water ripples moving sand dunes follow
white plumed body backwards happy
neck primed to suck a fly off surface.

Trumpeter Swan

Claws embed in dying bird flesh dripping
blood and liver morsels brooding watchful
screeches floating feathers settling cliffward.

Falcon

Pale cerulean cover clouds with bloodlust cackle
steel spikes slashing deeply into rabbit quiver
huge brown crossing peaks and whitecaps.

Golden Eagle

Blackened wing expanses stretching craw prongs
cradle deer head beaks a lover poised
to poke moist eyes sharing spoils making love.

Carrion Crow

Yellow claws clutch and lean away
from air stream joyful pipes to airborne
wind spans whirling over faded branch.

Black-winged Hawk

Turned away from sea cliff yearning
fledgling squawkers black and iron slivers
sparse crest move to hidden magnet wind rocks.

Great Cormorant

Webbed feet fern leaves clutch rock
brown and golden furry side rosettes
swelling doltish black-spot flowering eye-ring.

Horned Grebe

Six orange-headed white caw fly dead branches
bright green feathers move about conceiving leaves
at distance summer pecking hairy nuts.

Carolina Parakeet

Crest-hanging long white twists
wise considers distant farmer rice patch
yellow lances trample weed.

Snowy Heron

Barnacle molds adorning branches
beak thrust in beak thrust ensconcing kisses
feeding flap wings blissful yawn.

Passenger Pigeon

One web foot like white clam sucking black
hook-hanging eggshell beak, ballooning bellows
below bill shore-receded light house.

Brown Pelican

Black and white caught spreading action
water curve evading throat curve
open beak lands dead tree leaflessness.

Black-bellied Darter

Roseated wing expanse drips carmine deep
spoon bill wobbles claw-gripped rock decline
to gnat soup distant islands dreary.

Roseate Spoonbill

Night vitreous orbs yellow and question
in love with black in plume a thousand
birds in flight toward thickened nape.

Snowy Owl

Contented spiteful dissecting trout
open beak eye yellow glee beyond
river edge chopped cap white fly town.

Great White Heron

Black and pallid angel wings command
blench blue sky rough waters shriveled red legs
dangling steady taut dilapidated sea swells.

Black Skimmer

Pink-beak canopy on shore draws
over lesser bird isosceles carnelian
deeper than the water bleaching stand.

Scarlet Ibis

One slow red-legged paddles airborne snoot
green-quill cockade floating into lilies
one bullet flight aimed at marsh grass.

Red-breasted Merganser

Happy yellow compass comrade thrusting
back at turgid blue, darkly cobalt jets
ingot hanging wind endurance.

Great Blue Heron

Stream stepping craning open beak
unwary insect dark bar feathers
balance spawn in waded crest immobile.

Green Heron

Flaming solid crimson arch of neck
in taper shoulder wilting tail marsh
soak fellow splashing travelers.

American Flamingo

Yellow lining red smear blue smear yellow
white orb black top looking out befuddled
bloated white stripe grasses orange needle.

Atlantic Puffin

Cochineal seashell fear comb undergrowth
step softly craning pea-head panic perched
on purple candy-caned futility.

Wild Turkey

Long brown pods of honey-locust split
and seedless blackness pecks at bareness
clasps on pencil furling wing.

Fish Crow

One of many riding eastern hemlock
penetrating yellow bud other hanging
lanterns other flapping celebrations.

American Crossbill

Black oak's grandiose green and tawny
butterflies unaware of whip-poor whirring menace
set to pounce one already swallows colors.

Whip Poor Will

World-weary dark grasses blooming
blue and auburn wrinkles drowsy curving
neck descent to ancient eyes watching ruin.

California Vulture

Or instead a shining metal elongation
lusting, thrusting towards the sky,
blinding color abstract movement.

Bird in Space

Outside a Snowscape

Spruce shake second falling
    snow on snow

loved ones elsewhere take imagined drive
past house in which you lived for years
on brick blockades mutation stave acanthus
    untouched snow

lawn once a battlefield of toddler giggles
wayward snowball throws on hills blockade
unfurling white past bundled women walking
    windrow snow

glissade from room to room inside a mobile tent
to keep from touching other souls
to wither weeping storm alone
and billow whip above which no tree grows
behind a strip of bark shed dieback
    snow
    on snow on snow on snow

like Korak bundled bearskin cage
in larger tent of smoke taste reindeer
hair and tallow patch of moss to patch of moss
to stoned flesh die burn marrow floating
    over snow
    on snow on snow

on summer bittern's nest-bound warble
stain-glassed bluebird longing sky tent
roots through boulders into cascade
fondling flat rock lichen growth
of tiny emerald bushes twisting crazed
aloft from bark and waxy limegreen
embryonic cones on river water drying under toes
    on snow on snow

on other tents on other loved ones—
blank yester-snows
    on snow on snow

on photographs on window pane on blue ice
azo drips in baffle purse seine shrouded tent-like
    snow on snow
    on snow on snow

all of it outside of tent outside chimera prints
    in snow on snow on snow.

Weather is the Only Proof

      Heavy falling constant white sfumato
blurring distant vision
      whiter whirls above thin branches
tracing fishtail winds beneath ascending sky.

Concurrent fall and rise
      like all occurrence
            in the small

      random as the shape of snow

like all occurrence
      in ordinary scale
            of episode and dream

      floe and slope

like all occurrence in the large
      smooth and slowly
            encroaching or retreating

      ice's thick unscraping

occurrence as encounter
      snow as manna
            manna as occurrence

clear as wind's translucency

like all sky encounter
    wind chafing smoothness
        snow melting lip taste

    motion as manna

like proof of existence
    buckshot branches blurring sunless
        ascending sfumato occurrence

    fishtail as tracing hope.

Pascal's Triangle

In

a room

his Jonah murks

green stripes on wall like giant ribs

his black tea steeping like whale oil burning smoke the random sounds like

snore of leviathan wondering when he unbolts his dim cave will he empty onto terra firma or incognita where

what

one sees

not always now

hides a vacuum where the base of

an infinity lives in conic sections. Glimpse a single stalk.

Climb the bleached blue smoke of night falling quickly at a wounded shore. Gasp the clammy stench of aging pollen. Hear starling screeches as

caged

sound each

tone matrix as

weep. Feel bleeding where the cord cut

cramps of memory tricks. years ago from one who is now unspoken concealed from touch words Does that water cry in

Stare hours into the darkness of shut eyes toss hours trying to reenter the dream.

sleep

melt and

end before night

ends? Behind things are numbers of

this he is certain but behind the numbers behind the lines: space?

shapes? slowly dying therms? similes of his own bleak narcissism? beleaguered love or his steadfast craving? pure thought or the bare thing?

53

Protest Rock

Staff Meeting Minutes

Conference room, blah blah blanket walls dissolve
and flow, a plunge in frigid water, blah blah
beat of branches warms your tingling frozen flesh,
incorporated world between two walls of ice,
ha ha horses' heads on shivering human bodies,
da da disco rats merengue up the glacial switchback
seeking middens of your la la life to come,
discarded menus, transparent inhibitions,
a new caprice in permafrost: motes become beams,
rice becomes worms, wine becomes blood—ka ka
close your eyes, the paper angel wrestling you
is only you the times you win, another esker fantasy—
a higher I-don't-want-a wah wah want-to-be
until you reach that place that makes you smile:
walls become windows, glossy panes in bah bah bay.
The other side is summer, bathing ladies on parade,
like naked women always, beautiful and full of love.

What about the Losers?

What about the losers?,
second place or worse,
far from cheers and exultations
head in hand or pacing claustrophobia,
at least we played the game,
so close and yet so far:
if it wasn't for that hit, that swing,
bad hop, bad turn, bad call,
ball rolling off the fingertips,
fleeting lapse in concentration,
practiced my butt off, studied for years,
made the right moves, met the right people,
flattered, bantered, kissed their asses,
did without, planned ahead,
if it wasn't for contracting markets,
change in habits, insufficient cash flow,
someone with more contacts,
friend of brother, second cousin, old school tie,
secret handshake, lies and accusations,
loser, loser, loser, loser,
failure, lemon, flopperoo,
I don't want a stupid ribbon,
don't want the sloppy seconds,
second best, second hand,
greasy gruel at B-list parties,
legless wine, polyester fabric,
cloying banquet consolations,
finalist who never had a chance,

blew the chance I had,
never strong enough, never smart enough,
didn't work enough, wasn't hungry,
too small, too slow, too bored,
too lazy, too distracted, too fucked up,
I deserve to lose.

In the corner of an empty room
a lonely man constructs his fantasy:
a tree of life unfolding overhead
molting blue and silver leaves, each a coupon
for woman's love, exotic travel,
expensive cars, enormous houses.
He reaps his slips of paper,
presses them against his aging body
like a multicolored blanket
then stands up naked,
throws them to a rising wind
and watches as they drift and climb
toward ancient burnt-out stars,
scales his leafless tree,
jumps into the olive ocean,
swims to distant treeless coast
on which crowds of people cheer
for the joy of making noise.

Dreams of Old Men

I am fed up to the ears with old men dreaming up wars for young men to die in.
- George McGovern

War holy war necessary war beneficial war
war *amor patriae* war aurora borealis bound
war *a fortiori ad hoc ad interim ad infinitum* war.

War camp ground and carrion war plunder crops
war strip a city stop a tyrant free a people
war the cross war the book war the way.

Machete flesh, run a sword
through lungs and kidneys,

strangle plea to gurgle, rattle,
from a hilltop snipe off riders,

get in line to fuck the women of the dead,
one after another, one after another,

vibrate abstract Pollock gun swag
automatic blood-spray walls,

cockpit-monitor mushrooms,
pull switch-torch fire to hobbling bodies
blister skin, lather blood.

End impaled on sword
contemplating oozing entrails,
shiny curving viscous red,
delusions of pain:
my blood like floating temple roar,

in shivering swamp
gurgling fusty water
dry mouth sweating dysentery,
delusions of food:
wild boar and parsnips in stew,

jet imprisoned plunging snow
toward sultry ocean,
delusions of farewell:
ten nine eight long time left
six five four long time gone.

War holy war necessary war beneficial war
war *amor patriae* war aurora borealis bound
war *a fortiori ad hoc ad interim ad infinitum* war.

Ghost

Dreaming, soldiers lug me from the plane
despite my claims, American citizen,
blinded, neck between my knees,
ankles cuffed to wrists
motors whining, grumbling,
cars and planes and cars again.
Where am I? What did I do?
Why can't I call my wife?

I wake to driving my taxi.
Rocks explode the windshield.
I'm probing for damage
when soldiers engulf me,
sic leashed dogs, at my buttocks nipping,
cell me, strip me, chain me to a bed.
Booming trumpets ram my eardrums,
scorching flood lights detonate
dissolving eyelids, aching pupils.

I wake, moved to another cell,
wake again and moved again,
wake again and moved again,
wake and moved, wake and moved.

I wake to sear of burning cigarette
milled in ear, pushed to ground,
log-rolled over steaming excrement,
try to focus, pleasant memories,
wife and children, figs and coffee.

I wake hooded, naked
above another naked man
whose penis touches my rectum
below another naked man
whose rectum touches my penis
whose body's warmness teases me
to shameful reluctant erection.
Pulled from the pile, hood punched off,
I see a dozen hooded naked men
heaped to squalid pyramid of flesh
and a large gun pointed
by a soldier yelling, *Jerk off, hajji*
while a woman in soldier's garb
tapes my performance,
other soldiers laughing.

I wake submerged,
head held firmly underwater
by muscular ropes to boards,
ever louder squall of heart,
gasping, heaving, frenzied gurgles,
ever hotter burning crush of chest,
maiming claws at guts and lungs,
tingles creeping, penetrating every limb,
growing weary, fading, watery, confused …

I wake to tranquil breathing: my wife,
gentle whir: the dryer downstairs,
muffled roar: an SUV rumbling past our window.
The heavy pounding in my chest
gradually calms to regular beat
as I tell myself it was only a dream.

Gilgamesh in a Traffic Jam

Are you awake at steering column's crown
or sleeping on this crawl through disappearing
Andean glaciers, water towers of the world
transfigured over macadam to living
in the sadness of the premise of each herbal
tease fomenting muggy day outside
your fallopian ride from work?

When the pain of waking to another same-as-same-as
comes twist by twist, Swann-like, you never note
affliction or the neighbor boy asphyxiated
from the pass-out game, the fainting game,
the tingling FM rant tsunami first plague,
worldwide frog decline is number two
on hits parading past receded city,
West Nile Virus number three,
where do giant pouch rats fit?

Sometimes you try to guess the lives of others
when they signal exit cloverleaf to contemplate
in common suburb spongy swimming pools
coiled intestine faces humming bars of monstrous
concrete flag homology will search de Quincey's nisus:
meditate too much, observe too little.

The singularity of things material
evades Aquinine mindful dunning dread
no cause without an agent, nor agent without rebel,
phantasm action hero, Karna rides
his Mose-Jese Yama into Alabama, where
raven flights across the Volga publicize
the advent of utopian why-didn't-yous:
why didn't you go to Woodstock
with that halfway subway girl
when you were burger party Paul
with the one who let you touch her
driving through Encino on your
Thumbelina not her name,
but could have been, but here's your exit
and the kids want Wendy for their mom.

A Dream of Post-Historic Times

In the part of the brain that's a thousand
restless monkeys, prognosticators in genuflection
to themselves elect a representative to the welkin world
where love is tinsel whelk come to wheat worm
butterflied, sautéed, served on sesame bungle
up your season tickets good for gala openings
of gallerias and millenarian exfoliation
around the mitochondria, occasionally well-schooled
in fixing results of presidential pneumectomies.
Do they eat with their knees or with dead branches
left from moving rivers named no clue, no sale,
no way to *sic erat in fatis seriatim,* broadly speaking
and subject to recall: steam cleaners that hemorrhage
scalding water, security cameras cracking
at the mount assembly, falling hazard, pacemakers
seeping moisture, shocking hearts to overdrive,
people you admire who pick their noble savage,
see-through shrimp in towering mineral chimneys
blowing numen seeking salmon trout and salsa salpingo
doesn't hear the warning signs inside the mask of naming.

Faith is a Fine Invention

Faith is a fine invention, for gentlemen who see
But microscopes are prudent in an emergency!
- Emily Dickinson

Faith gropes a button,
expects a door to open.

Faith rebuilds a house
on warm lava. Faith counts steps
eyes closed along a sidewalk.

Faith photographs herself
naked in the bedroom light
with a young man she just met.

Faith chants a blessed name
in a mountain temple. Faith mutters
prayers before and after eating.

Faith talks to candles. Faith pores
over ancient texts seeking insight,
accepts a life of indigence. Faith buys

overvalued equities. Faith believes
a future generation will fabricate machines
to clean degraded air. Faith draws

a white hood over head,
sets a torch ablaze. Faith destroys
the books and monuments

of other cultures. Faith sends men
into ditches filled with water
and the stench of rats. Faith signs

commands to blast explosives
over foreign cities, flies the planes
and drops the bombs.

Faith lets doctors pump poison
into veins and throws up breakfast
in a pail beside the bed.

Faith sees ragged pieces,
a puzzle depicting night,
and calls it day. Faith is

a black box with hidden switches.
Faith delights in moments
soaked with giddy joy

when flowing atmosphere and moving branch
create a buzz of bliss, and life appears
to stop in springtime's murmur

not to move again.

Variations on a Ballad

Will we remember
that Douglas Leigh arranged Broadway lights
into scalding cups of coffee, fishes blowing bubbles,
giant dancing couples,

Nathan Handwerker
ladled kraut and relish
over dogs in steaming buns
to lovers and families outside
bumper cars in Coney Island,

Jacob Kaplan
gave away his millions made by selling juice
to house abused and homeless,

A. N. Spanel
invented pneumatic stretchers, plastic girdles,
won a libel suit versus Westbrook Pegler?

Will we remember
Mario Savio raising his voice,

Albert Maltz refusing to answer,

Salvator Altcheck,
nonagenarian creaking up stairs, his five-buck house calls,

Alfred Hershey fiercely shaking
viral soup in kitchen blenders counting parts in DNA,

Monte Miller
who told his cult that Satan's spawn
revealed to him the date of earth's destruction,

that boy whose parents
pretended he had genius, did his homework
so he could graduate at ten,

that guy who served
six years in jail for rape before his accuser
admitted she lied to keep her dad from beating her,

the twin girls creating a private language
that no one else could understand,

the roller derby queen
called The Blonde Bomber,

the parents who baby-sat virtual pets?

Will we remember Viktor Frankl's
Man's Search for Meaning,
the chapter on prison routine,

Grace Paley's essay on the thirties,

Sankai Juku sand storm plunging floorwards,

Laura Nyro singing Stone Soul Picnic,

Molly Picon shining shoes in Yiddle
with a Fiddle,

John Fahey dithering his guitar,

Morris Carnovsky as Lear?

Will we
remember Al DeRogatis predicting
a screen from Starr to Taylor,

Mo Lucas jumping for the ball,
elbows over heads of all the other players,

Whoopie Creedon, White Wings Tebeau,
the Goose, the Whammy, Heinie Meine,

the photo in the New York Times
of Berra, Bauer, Moose and Whitey
arriving together for Mickey's interment?

Will we remember Mean Joe Greene
tossing his jersey and fondling a Coke,

the fast-talking man rapidly explaining
if it absolutely positively has to get there …

the old lady looking up suspiciously,
a finger deep in burger bun and asking,
Where's the beef?

California raisins
shuffling to soul,

Bartles and James
sitting on a porch and drinking sweetened wine,

a hilltop choir wanting to teach the world to sing,

Mikey, Speedy, Joe Isuzu, spicy meatball?

Will we
remember John Daly teasing Dorothy Kilgallen,

Bob Barker barking *Come on down,*

Alex Trebek
reading answers, asking for questions,

Vanna flipping letters,

Paul Lynde twisting
entendres cross his lips like unlit cigarettes?

Will we remember Disney's gated city,
Beetles tribute bands, religious-based mutual funds,
energy and fitness drinks, outlet malls, Y2K?

Will
we remember the meaning of make it real,
park that thought, psychic power tools,
taking a quick scuba in the think tank,

I have the ball, warm and fuzzy,
kidvid sudser tubthump moppet macho
hyper blurb at this point in time
unplugged cyber ethnic cleansing
been there done that colorized wellness?

                    Will we remember
the first shallow snow of callous winter,
the first purple crocus yearning skyward,
the first firefly landing on a rhododendron,
illuminating a broad leaf briefly
then silently announcing its version of darkness?

Songs of Self

Again in L. A.

Fifty-six in a twenty-five, curve on curve,
    escarp through canyon granite,
        swaying wild and yellow flowers,

    panoramic swipes of green and tan,
windows opened, radio sings
  Life's been good to me so far.

    You've been here before
  and will be back again,
will drive back, will drive by,

    will lay back, will fly by,
      will chill and flow, sun and fun,
  embrace and be embraced

by desiccated vibes propelling
  warm across a twelve-lane highway;

    elastic parking lots enticing you
to leave your cold and turned-on shell
rolling slowly towards the bougainvillea of the valley.

Apollo

- for Michael Herschensohn

Vicious dragon eating prostate,
    I will slay it,

blast spears of plague at evil's camp,
    guide arrows into scourge's heel.

Boa choking life, I will feed it
    tiny metal seeds dehiscing radiation,

my ambrosia and nectar,
    beauty, healing, light.

I become the sun,
    my pyknic being radiates,

I glow from pleasure's pith
    outward towards all creatures.

I want to charm the world,
    warm it with albedo bounces,

chase life, Apollo chasing Daphne,
    hopelessly full of hope,

full of dawn, porch-rocked exhaustion
    imposing reason, harmony,

gleaming rainbeams from a burnt-out star,
    coruscating clouds and birds

too far away to burn
       babes and pregnant women,

a floating island watching
       world through crusted canthi.

My flow of unabridged desire
       creates a sacred grove of every day

madrona, cascara, ladyfern
       now Apollo's hyacinth and palm,

the people passing by
       now holy swan and dolphin,

stray sounds now a singing stream,
       lyric chants of blessed life,

a dream that seems so real
       I won't remember it.

The Sixth Dream of Gilgamesh

...on the face of the river on [...]
    a day dead outnumber living [...]
[...] frightened man [...] stabbing at me, missing
    [...] I keep dialing the wrong number,

my fingers moving faster than I can [...]
    and when I get it right, no one answers [...]
[...] falling from the tower, shouting...
    [...] it wasn't [...] my fault [...] in a thousand

[...] different tongues [...] shaped like chanterelle
    under oak in rotting leaves [...]
into rivers of panthers, vessels of lions [...]
    [...] believing their prayers [...]

[...] across the field holding hands [...]
    everyone I ever met [...] forgiving [...]
[...] me [...] the mountain is a baying
    golden calf [...] thirteen winds darken [...]

[...] the tower begins to dance
    and the sky implores the mountain
not abandon it [...] not yet [...]
    There is no explanation.

Ravings of an Atheistic Stylite

Drift all is drift,
nomads in sandstorm at edges of empire,
dustbowl of animated fragments
that banish/varnish the past,
the creeping barchan's Brownian tango
replicates/inculcates/suffocates
with passionless freedom's wandering eye
when meditator is meditation.

Drift all is drift all is lift Bernoulli
tooling through the drooling clouds
cross-legged squat on distant pillar
in the clenches on the beaches
up on the roof under the bored walker
save the last drift for sliding under
iced Beringian lineage seeking mastodon
on ether/netherworld in driftdream:
you didn't have to be so drift,
I would have drifted anyway.

Drift all is drift all is flux
all is spate is pile is clump
is spending and accumulation
collect/let go/fret and set
a grifter's gift in downshift sift
of spendthrift swift-kick miffed
at drift all is drift.

Drift's Notes:
cloud in sky, leaf in rake,
ice on water, caribou in woodland,
ballooning spider casting trembling gossamer,
tectonic plates on upper mantle,
dye in teardrops, throw of die,
disorderly ideas, planetary traveler,
Milky Way's expanding chaos,
times to come before they happen,
lust for beauty, memory in dementia,
a mind immersed in saxophone or booze,
eyeless will in drift all is drift.

Schoenberg's Second Conversion

When I was a boy, they told me,
submerge your head in water, count to ten.
Instead I counted heartbeats and there were twelve
and I made my song.

I dreamed of Jacob's ladder,
angels flying upward, angels flying downward twelve rungs,
each a tribe, I thought, or perhaps a tone
and I wanted to raise my song.

There is one temple in heaven that only music opens
and for it I searched, dragging my twelve tribes of sound,
the modern Jacob, I thought, whose children are syllogisms
giving birth to law, giving birth to song.

Rung by rung, learning what I knew,
posing a problem, then solving and re-solving,
then seeking a precept behind all solution
until I had climbed twelve rungs and prayed my song.

Now, fleeing Hitler in this month of fire,
I listen for the law of sound in the train's blunt rasp
and read of Jacob's dream and understand my blunder:
The ladder is beside him, but he does not climb.

When the train stops, it will be Paris
and I will disembark and find a ritual bath
and dunk myself a second time and, head submerged,
count heartbeats till twelve, and this time
the song will make me.

One of Repin's Volga Boatmen

Inside whites and yellows, one of many haulers
dragging bandaged feet through sand, hearing casing
scrape against the river bottom, first as soothing
wave-like slurping, then as gritty soldier's song,
squall of waking succubus, endless drone,
sun-like thrashing, slicing into pulling back,
a dream of timeless towing, pilgrim rags and sweat
tug the flattened road, admire the landscape
chasing river trances into embryonic winter wheat,
heavy rain descending like the ending of the world,
this hour of hauling crashes with the next,
this day devours itself in dying weir.

Awaken as another hauler, not the one
who drinks his milk on fast days, nor he
who seeks in fuse of chant with flesh
flight from worthlessness, not he who carries
water, bread and salt across the steppes,
sleeps outside and hides in secret rooms,
nor the one parading nude before the court,
nor whacking bloody welts on back and legs.
I am a merchant on the way to colder regions
exploring underwater kingdoms for truths
I can keep and also barter, washing ashore
with golden fish in an unknown land.

Notes

July Fourth
Joe Venuti, the first great jazz violinist, began performing before 1920.

Dot and Sylvia
Sylvia is Sylvia Plath. The poem quotes three lines from her poem Ariel.

These are a Few
John Coltrane on his death bed reviews his life in a sax-like word solo.

Showing off the Roses
Substantia nigra is a layer of deeply pigmented gray matter in the midbrain, and is the part of the brain most affected by Parkinson's disease.

Hugo Speaks to Himself and Emmy speaks to Hugo
Hugo Ball and Emmy Hennings first coined the term Dada.

Imaginary Landscape with 29 Birds (After Audubon)
In 2004, the University of Pittsburgh's Frick Fine Arts Museum asked me to write a poem about its exhibition of Audubon bird prints and include it in a reading. The first 28 stanzas of the poem each describe a specific bird Audubon painted. The 29th bird is Brancusi's sculpture, *Bird in Space*.

Variations on a Ballad
This poem renovates and expands Francois Villon's *Ballade des dames du temps jadis*.

The Sixth Dream of Gilgamesh

On his journey to fight the giant Humbaba, Gilgamesh has five dreams, all of which his friend, Enkidu, interprets as good omens.

Pascal's Triangle

The lines of the poem are arranged to represent the beginning of four Pascal Triangles. Pascal's Triangle is a pyramid of numbers arranged in rows consisting of the coefficients in the expansion of $(a + b)n$ for n .0,1,2,3... In simple English, the number directly below two numbers is the sum of the two everywhere on every row:

$$
\begin{array}{ccccccc}
 & & & 1 & & & \\
 & & 1 & & 1 & & \\
 & & 1 & 2 & 1 & & \\
 & 1 & 3 & 3 & 1 & & \\
 1 & 4 & 6 & 4 & 1 & & \\
1 & 5 & 10 & 10 & 5 & 1 &
\end{array}
$$

In the poem, I use clusters of syllables to represent these rows, as follows:
Row one: One cluster of one syllable
Row two: Two clusters of one syllable
Row three: Three clusters of one, two and one syllables, respectively
Row four: Four clusters of one, three, three and one syllables, respectively
And so on.

While mathematicians have created these triangles for millennia, it was the French scientist and philosopher, Blaise Pascal, who uncovered most of its beautifully poetic mathematical eccentricities. Some examples:

The triangular numbers (bowling pin totals, or 1, 3, 6, 10, 15...) can be found in the diagonal starting at row 3. If a diagonal of numbers of any length is selected starting at a one bordering the triangle and ending on any number inside the triangle on that diagonal, the sum of the numbers inside the selection is equal to the number below the end of the selection not on the same diagonal itself. Fibonacci sequences can also be located in another pattern. This short list does not begin to exhaust the abundant mathematical delights of Pascal's Triangle.

The persistent reader will find correspondences to these mathematical patterns in diagonal and other geometric readings of the poem's syllable clusters. In this way, one can contrive completely different poems, all expressing multiple layers of meaning pointed thematically in the same general directions.

Photo by Michael Ray

Marc Jampole was born in 1950 in New York City. He earned a Bachelor of Arts (Honors) from the University of Wisconsin-Milwaukee and a Master of Arts from the University of Washington, both in comparative literature. He also conducted independent research at the University of Berlin, Germany, on a Fulbright Fellowship. Marc has worked professionally as a television news reporter, filmmaker, university instructor, options trader and writer. He has written more than 350 articles on various subjects for magazines and newspapers.

Marc's poetry has been published in *Mississippi Review, Oxford Review, Janus Head, Ellipsis, Main Street Rag* and other journals. *Oxford Review* nominated one of his poems for *The Pushcart Prize*.